MIND VS. MUSCLE

THE PSYCHOLOGY OF SPORTS

HOCKEY

CATHLEEN SMALL

Gareth Stevens
PUBLISHING

Please visit our website, **www.garethstevens.com**.
For a free color catalog of all our high-quality books,
call toll free 1-800-542-2595 of fax 1-877-542-2596.

Cataloging-in-Publication Data

Names: Small, Cathleen.
Title: Hockey / Cathleen Small.
Description: New York : Gareth Stevens Publishing, 2019. | Series: Mind vs muscle: the
psychology of sports | Includes glossary and index.
Identifiers: LCCN ISBN 9781538225394 (pbk.) | ISBN 9781538225486 (library bound)
Subjects: LCSH: Hockey--Juvenile literature.
Classification: LCC GV847.25 S63 2019 | DDC 796.962--dc23

First Edition

Published in 2019 by
Gareth Stevens Publishing
111 East 14th Street, Suite 349
New York, NY 10003

© 2019 Gareth Stevens Publishing

Produced for Gareth Stevens by Calcium Creative Ltd
Editors: Sarah Eason and Jennifer Sanderson
Designers: Paul Myerscough and Simon Borrough
Picture researcher: Rachel Blount

Picture credits: Cover: Shutterstock: Iurii Osadchi; Inside: Shutterstock: Agusyonok:
p. 12; Mitrofanov Alexander: p. 15; B Calkins: p. 34; Ronnie Chua: p. 17; Dotshock: pp. 20,
31; Eric Fahrner: p. 32; Stan Fin: p. 13; Fotokvadrat: pp. 26–27; Steve Gilbert: p. 29; Marcel
Jancovic: p. 16; John-Alex: p. 18; Jonah_H: p. 43; Kat72: p. 11; Katatonia82: p. 45; Kovop58:
p. 10; Lucky Business: pp. 9, 23; Boiarkina Marina: p. 40; Sergey Mironov: pp. 38, 39, 42;
Mopic: p. 4; Muzsy: p. 22; Sergey Nivens: p. 44; Robert Nyholm: pp. 35, 36, 41; Eugene
Onischenko: pp. 1, 6; Iurii Osadchi: p. 30; Pe3k: p. 24; Luca Santilli: p. 21; Shooter Bob
Square Lense: p. 33; Daniel M. Silva: p. 37; Bonma Suriya: pp. 5, 25; Laszlo Szirtesi: p.8;
Adam Vilimek: p. 14; Andrey Yurlov: p. 28; Leonard Zhukovsky: p. 19; Wikimedia
Commons: Aaron Frutman: p. 7.

Printed in the United States of America

CPSIA compliance information: Batch #CS18GS:
For further information contact Gareth Stevens, New York, New York, at 1-800-542-2595.

CONTENTS

CHAPTER 1

THE PSYCHOLOGY OF

When playing sports with friends, the main aim of the game is usually to have fun. Anyone can play, no matter what their skill level. But when sports become competitive, **athleticism** is very important. The more athletic the players, the better they will do in the sport.

However, games or matches are not won based on pure brawn or athletic skill. They are won by people who understand the mental strategy needed to win. Players need to understand the strategy behind the sport.

Many athletes use psychology to help develop their understanding of strategy, as well as to improve their play on the field, on the court, in the pool, or on the ice. Psychology in general is used to help people better understand their own motivations. It is also used to teach people to manage stress and adopt a positive mind-set before a big event, such as a game.

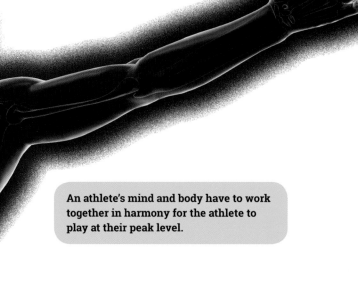

An athlete's mind and body have to work together in harmony for the athlete to play at their peak level.

Psychologists can teach people effective techniques to accomplish all their goals. There are also dedicated sports psychologists, who help athletes achieve these goals to enhance their performance.

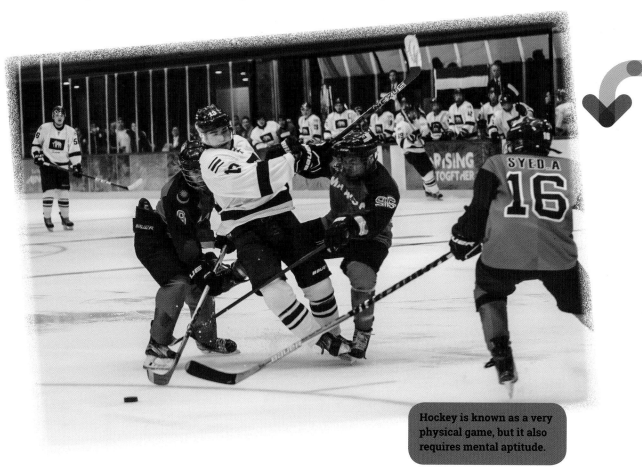

Hockey is known as a very physical game, but it also requires mental aptitude.

WHAT IS SPORTS PSYCHOLOGY?

The field of sports psychology began in the late 1800s, when psychologist Norman Triplett studied cyclists. Triplett found that cyclists performed better when they rode as a group than when they trained as individuals. In 1925, psychologist Coleman Griffith set up the first sports psychology laboratory at the University of Illinois. At the same time, other psychologists were working in the field, too, at universities such as Stanford in California. Today, the field continues to grow, and most major sports teams rely on sports psychology techniques to help their players achieve their best performance.

The field of sports psychology looks at how psychology affects sports performance, as well as how participating in sports affects an athlete's mental state. Sports psychologists teach coaches and players techniques, such as **arousal regulation, visualization, goal setting**, and **self-talk**, to help players improve their performance.

Plays like this happen when the player's mind is on the game and the player is completely focused on the task at hand.

ALL IN THE MIND

Bobby Orr: Realistic Goals and Motivation

Canada's Bobby Orr is widely considered one of the best hockey players of all time. Over the course of 12 years, from 1966 to 1978, he played defense for the Boston Bruins and the Chicago Blackhawks. On the ice, he was fast, smart, and good at scoring. His reputation earned him a spot in the Hockey Hall of Fame as the youngest player ever to be inducted up to that point. He also holds the record for the most points and assists in a single season by a defensive player.

Although Orr was a defensive player, he was known for playing very offensively. He could skate incredibly fast, and he would rush to wherever the puck was and go for it, rather than hanging back like many defensive players. Orr says he did not want to sit back—he wanted to be involved, and if that meant playing offensively as a defenseman, then that is what he did.

Orr found motivation during National Hockey League (NHL) seasons by segmenting the season into 10-game chunks. He would then challenge himself to play at his peak ability for 8 games of each 10-game segment. He would cut himself a little slack for the other two games, since realistically, no one can be in perfect physical shape for every single game.

While it might be tempting to set a goal such as, "I will play at the top of my ability in every game," it would not be realistic. Hockey is a tough sport, and no one can play at their peak in every game. By setting more manageable, but still ambitious goals, Orr was able to keep up his motivation and become one of the best players professional hockey has ever seen.

Hockey legend Bobby Orr set realistic goals to try to constantly improve his performance on the ice.

PSYCHOLOGY IN HOCKEY

In the early days of hockey, the sport was played on frozen ponds in Canada. While some say that hockey as a team sport was first played in the United Kingdom, most historians agree that it was more widely played and formalized in Canada in the late 1800s, with professional ice hockey beginning around 1900. It was, from the beginning, a tough sport for the strongest players.

Cal Botterill, a former Canadian hockey player who is now a sports psychologist, says that the **subculture** of hockey is very different from other sports. He describes how the subculture came from the pioneering spirit of the early Canadians, whom he said had to be obsessively competitive in order to thrive and survive. Canadians thought it was essential for men to be tough, persistent, and able to defend themselves. Hockey players are most definitely tough—it is a rough sport.

Physical toughness is a cornerstone of hockey philosophy.

Even young hockey players recognize the importance of strategy on the ice.

Botterill says that out of this subculture, the hockey value system of winning at any cost came about. In all team sports, mental strategy is important. Players must use strategy for their own play, but they must also apply that strategy to what is best for the team. In hockey, the team is particularly important. It is a rough game, and teams are known to be very protective of their players. Sometimes, players will continue playing when they are injured, if they think that strategy will best help their team win.

Hockey relies on a strategy that the best way to win is to put the team above all else. Sports psychologists work with hockey players to help them **internalize** that team unity. They also help players build confidence, enter the right mind-set for play, and set goals that will enable them to perform to the best of their ability.

CHAPTER 2

THE BASICS OF
Hockey

Hockey has been around for more than 100 years. To understand the mental strategies that have been developed around the sport, it is helpful to understand what hockey looked like in its early days, as well as the basics of how and where hockey is played.

THE EARLY DAYS OF HOCKEY

In some countries, field hockey is more common than ice hockey, but in the United States and Canada, if a person says "hockey," they are almost certainly talking about ice hockey.

Hockey was originally played on frozen lakes and ponds, and it often still is!

The earliest games of hockey were played with sticks and balls in the United Kingdom, but hockey as we know it developed in Canada and had the same basic setup as today's game. Players used sticks and a puck, and the object was to score by hitting the puck into the opposing team's goal.

It is reported that in the very earliest days of outdoor hockey, pucks were actually chunks of frozen cow dung. In the first organized indoor hockey game—held in Montreal, Canada, in 1875—the puck was made of wood instead of rubber. The teams had nine players each instead of six, and the goals were 8 feet (2.4 m) wide instead of 6 feet (1.8 m) wide. Although there were minor differences from today, the overall game and strategy were the same.

Hockey quickly became very popular. By 1893, there were nearly 100 teams in the Montreal area, and certain strategies and plays were beginning to be developed. One such play was the scoop shot. In the scoop, the puck is lifted off the ice, and travels in the air for a short distance. Scoop shots are useful when the player wants to lift the puck over another player's head, such as over the goaltender's head and into the goal.

As hockey became more popular, outdoor rinks were created.

In cold climates, hockey lovers often gather on frozen ponds to play pickup games.

THE LOCATION

In its simplest form, hockey is played on ice—any ice. It can be a formal hockey rink or arena, or it can be as simple as a frozen pond or lake. Sometimes, in very cold regions, people will even flood a flat area of land, such as in their yard, and allow it to freeze over to create a makeshift ice rink. To play a pickup game of hockey, all that is needed is a decent-size patch of ice and some basic equipment.

A formal hockey rink is usually inside an arena. It is generally rectangular with rounded corners. The rink is surrounded by the boards, which are walls approximately 3.5 to 4 feet (1–1.2 m) tall. The size of a hockey rink depends on where it is and what it is being used for. The rinks in North America are referred to as NHL rinks, and they are slightly smaller than the Olympic rink used in the rest of the world. NHL rinks are usually 200 feet (61 m) long and 85 feet (26 m) wide. They have a corner **radius** of 28 feet (8.5 m). It is 11 feet (3.3 m) from the end boards to the nearest goal line. NHL rinks also have expanded the attacking zones over Olympic rinks; the blue lines are 64 feet (19.5 m) from the **icing** line (or goal line) and 50 feet (15.2 m) apart.

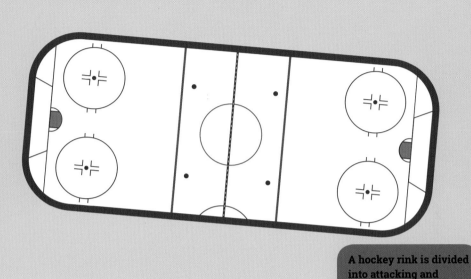

A hockey rink is divided into attacking and defending zones.

ICE MARKINGS

The thick blue lines are two of the five lines on a professional hockey rink, and the center red line divides the rink in half crosswise. The icing lines are located on each end of the rink, right where the goals are, which is why they are also sometimes known as goal lines. Between the icing lines and the center red line are the blue lines.

The blue lines are used to determine when a player is **offside**. The center line is used to determine icing. The blue lines also serve to divide the rink into three zones. On each end, between the icing line and the blue line is the defending zone or defensive zone. That same zone is also the attacking zone or offensive zone—it just depends what team is in it. For the team defending its goal, that zone is the defending zone. For the team attempting to score, that zone is the attacking zone. Collectively, the attacking/defending zones are known as end zones. Between the two blue lines (and encompassing the center red line), the zone is known as the neutral zone. It is also sometimes called center ice.

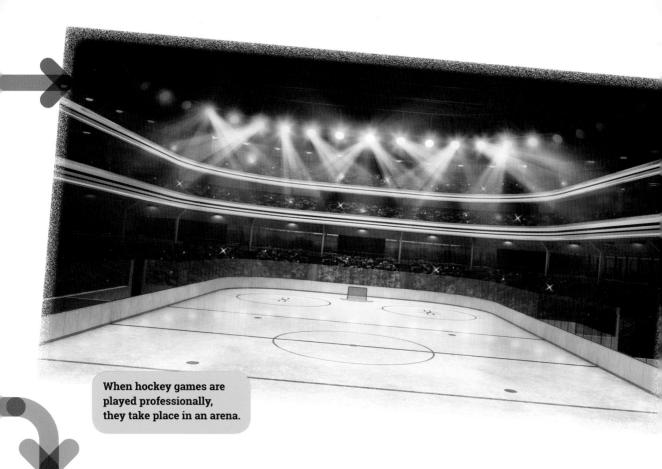

When hockey games are played professionally, they take place in an arena.

The Olympic rinks used around the world follow International Ice Hockey Federation (IIHF) specifications. They are the same length as NHL rinks, but they are wider at 98.4 feet (30 m). Their corner radius is also the same as NHL rinks, but their attacking zones are slightly smaller. Instead of the blue lines being 64 feet (19.5 m) from the icing line, they are 61.9 feet (18.9 m) from the icing lines.

All rinks have nine **face-off** spots. These spots are where face-offs take place. There are four spots in the neutral zone, two spots in each attacking/defending end zone, and one at center ice. The spots at center ice and in the end zones have circles or **hash marks** painted around them, to show where players can position themselves during a face-off.

Each end of the rink has a metal goal frame with a net. This is where the attacking team must shoot the puck to earn points. There is a semicircular area around the goal called the crease. This is the goaltender's territory. If an attacking player enters the crease with his stick, skate, or any body part before the puck enters the area, the goal will not count.

14

THE POSITIONS

Six players are on the ice at any given time for a hockey team. One player is the goaltender, or goalie. The goaltender's job is to protect the goal. The five other players skate up and down the ice trying to score goals. These five other players have positions somewhat similar to those in soccer. There are three offensive players: the center, the right wing, and the left wing, and there are two defensive players: the right defenseman and the left defenseman.

THE EQUIPMENT

Hockey is well known as a dangerous sport because of the injuries that can happen. The rubber puck moves at high speed, sometimes in the air, and can easily cause harm if a player is hit by it. Ice is slippery, and collisions between players often occur—sometimes purposely, as part of game play. The blades on hockey skates are sharp and can easily cut another player. Hockey players carry sticks that can also cause injury.

Referees ensure that games do not become too dangerous, which is possible despite all the protective gear worn by players.

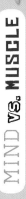

SHIFTING PERSPECTIVE:
THE OFFENSIVE DEFENSEMAN

Hockey is such a fast-moving game that it is not unusual for the players to find themselves playing both offense and defense. Many consider hockey to be a game of transitions—players are always transitioning, or changing, between offensive and defensive play. The coach of the 1994 U.S. Olympic men's hockey team, Tim Taylor, once commented that the key to hockey is the offensive defenseman—that is, the defenseman who can turn defensive play into offense.

Ken Dryden, author and former NHL goaltender, spoke about how useful the ability to transition between offense and defense can be. Dryden wrote that before offense turns to defense or vice versa, there is a moment of disequilibrium, when the team's defense is vulnerable. The opposing team can use this moment to its advantage. He says that the clever hockey player, the offensive defenseman, sees this opportunity and seizes it.

The best hockey players can switch rapidly between offense and defense.

Helmets, gloves, and skates are a part of any hockey player's wardrobe.

Unsurprisingly, hockey players wear a lot of protection to keep them safe from hazards. All players are required to wear a rigid plastic helmet that is padded on the inside. Helmets reduce the risk of head injuries. Often, players wear a face cage or visor as part of their helmet. This protects their face and head from injuries as a result of sticks or flying pucks.

Hockey players also wear padded, puncture-resistant neck guards that help reduce the risk of pucks, sticks, or skate blades causing neck injuries. They usually wear mouthguards to protect their teeth and jaw. Without a face cage and mouthguard, jaw fractures and knocked-out teeth are not uncommon.

Shoulder pads are also important equipment for hockey players. They protect not just the players' shoulders, but also the chest, ribs, spine, and **solar plexus** from collisions and flying pucks. Elbow pads protect the elbows, forearms, and sometimes the **triceps**. Bruises and bone fractures are common in hockey, and elbow pads can help protect against those.

Hockey players wear special hockey skates. While figure skates have a little claw on the front of the blade known as a toe pick, hockey skates do not have this pick. They have a rounded heel, too. The rounded heel and lack of a toe pick is much safer when there is a pileup of players on the ice. Hockey skates have foam insides to conform to the player's feet, but on the outside, the skates are hard plastic with rigid toe caps and heel protectors.

Players use a stick that is made of wood, graphite, or a **composite** material. There is no standard stick size for regulation play—instead, the stick length depends on the player's height.

The hockey puck is made of vulcanized rubber, which is very hard. It is 3 inches (8 cm) in diameter and 1 inch (2.5 cm) thick. It weighs 6 ounces (170 g). The players use their sticks to propel the puck across the ice and hopefully into the goal.

The puck may be small, but it can cause a lot of damage if it hits a person or object.

Hockey jerseys have the team's colors and **logo** on them, as well as the player's name and number on the back. Having names and numbers helps the referee—and in professional games, the commentators—identify the players.

UNIFORMS

Players' shoulder and elbow pads are covered with a jersey. The jersey has the team's colors and logo on it, as well as the player's name and number on it. Just as in many other sports, professional and competitive hockey teams may have slightly different jerseys depending on whether they are playing a home or an away game. One unique piece of a hockey jersey is the fight strap, which connects the jersey to the inside of the player's pants. It is required in professional leagues, because sometimes, players will try to pull an opponent's jersey over their head during play. Hockey pants are knee-length and include pads for the thigh, pelvis, hip, and tailbone. They are sometimes held up by a belt or suspenders.

Hockey socks are big and held up by **garters**. They cover the shin guards, which are padding for the shins and the knee. Shin guards have a hard plastic front to protect players' shins from strikes by the puck or a stick, but there is no coverage on the calf.

13

Goalies have extra protective gear and slightly modified skates and sticks.

THE GOALTENDER'S EQUIPMENT

The goaltender has slightly different equipment from the rest of the players on the team. Their stick generally has a larger blade and a wider, flat shaft than that of other players. Goaltenders' sticks are almost always made of wood, and they are designed for better impact resistance, since they have to stop fast-moving pucks.

The goalie's skates tend to have a thicker-than-normal blade and less ankle support. This is because the goalie needs some increased maneuverability to stop the puck. The blade of the skate is also usually closer to the skate boot, so that the puck cannot slide into the goal by going through the narrow area between the boot and the blade. This sounds impossible, but it does sometimes happen with normal skates.

Goalies also wear more protective face masks, helmets, and neck guards than other players. During a 1989 NHL game, a player's skate blade sliced the neck of Canadian goalie Clint Malarchuk, causing severe blood loss from his **carotid artery** and **jugular vein**. After this life-threatening injury, many NHL goalies began to wear neck protection.

Catch gloves, or trappers, help the goalie catch the puck.

The padding worn by goalies is more concentrated in the front and lighter in the back. This is because goalies are nearly always facing the puck and opposing players. However, padding becomes heavy and very hot, so often, padding on the back is sacrificed to keep the weight and temperature down for the goalie. Goal pads, which are worn on the legs, are the most heavily padded piece of goalie equipment. These pads are so large and thick that they are used to block many shots into the goal, in what is called a pad stop.

Goalies wear a blocker on their stick-holding hand. This is a glove with a pad on the back that can be used to deflect shots on the goal. On their other hand, the goalie wears a catch glove or trapper, which is used to help catch the puck on the ice or in the air.

CHAPTER 3

COACHING AND TEAM
Strategies

Hockey is a unique sport in that it requires mastery of hockey skills, such as hitting the puck with the stick, and also basic skating skills. In other team sports, such as football, basketball, and soccer, players already know how to run because it is something they have been doing since they were young children. However, skating is not a skill taught to all children, so in some cases, a coach's first strategy is to make sure the players master the basic skill of skating. Once players have learned the basics, coaches can work on other strategies to build a strong team.

As in any team sport, the coach is very important in building team unity.

Coaches work to build players' focus on the ice, where it's needed during a fast-paced game.

BUILDING FOCUS

There is a lot going on in a hockey game. Research has shown that people who try to do more than one task at a time are not as productive as those who focus on one task at a time. Good hockey coaches know this and do not try to give the players too many instructions during games.

Hockey is a fast-paced game, and the players' brains are already challenged by trying to process what is happening on the ice and adjusting their strategy based on that. If they have the added pressure of a coach screaming instructions from the sidelines, it only makes the processing more difficult.

The best coaches will save their coaching for practice or time-outs, to avoid distracting their players. They also work with players on strategies to block out distractions and focus on their task. One strategy some coaches use for this is self-talk. They teach players a word or phrase they can say to themselves to direct their attention to the task at hand and block out everything else.

ALL IN THE MIND

Herb Brooks: Miracle on Ice

According to *Sports Illustrated*, the top sports moment in the twentieth century was hockey's "Miracle on Ice." At the 1980 Winter Olympics in Lake Placid, New York, the U.S. hockey team was playing against the Soviet Union team, which had won six gold medals in the previous seven Olympic games. The U.S. team was young and inexperienced, and the Soviets were heavily favored to win. In the third period of the game, the United States were down 3–2, but they came back and scored two goals, winning the game. They went on to beat Finland in the final game, which won the very young team the Olympic gold medal.

Although some did not expect the young team to perform well, coach Herb Brooks had used a psychological strategy when he put together the team. He asked players to answer a 300-question psychological test that would show him how they would react under stress. He knew that the best team would be made up of players who could perform well under pressure, and he built the team with that strategy in mind.

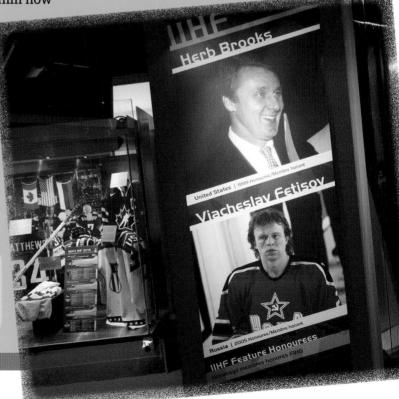

"Miracle on Ice" was such a pivotal moment that movies and documentaries have been made about it.

Being able to read the game can make the difference between winning and losing a face-off.

READING THE SITUATION

Although hockey has many plays and planned strategies that are used in every game, much of the game is spent reacting to unexpected events and changing plans. Hockey games move fast, because on ice, the players and the puck move faster than they would on a field or a court. No matter how skilled a hockey player is, ice can be unpredictable. The puck may end up in an entirely different place on the rink from where it was intended to go.

The best hockey coaches will spend time teaching players to read the situation and react to it. They focus on instinct in the fast-moving game; they teach players to follow their own instinct and visualize where they and the puck need to go.

Using visualization is a common sports psychology strategy. It works as mental practice. The player might not actually be performing the actions physically at that moment, but they are practicing for it by performing in their brain. It is also known to be a way to build confidence in athletes, because in their mind, they see themselves succeeding at their task.

MAXIMIZING INTENSITY

Hockey is an incredibly demanding sport. It requires speed, strength, and physical **intensity**. Coaches try to maximize players' intensity to make sure they perform at their peak. One sports psychology technique that helps them do this is arousal regulation.

Hockey players must be in a highly intense state to perform well on the ice.

Arousal regulation does not always mean getting more intense. Sometimes, it is just the opposite. Sometimes, even in hockey, coaches will notice that players are too intense—they are nervous and unlikely to play well. So, coaches will use relaxation, **meditation**, and breathing exercises to try to calm nervous players.

On the other hand, if coaches need to motivate relaxed players to get their energy up, they might play upbeat music or do other exercises designed to energize the players. All of these are arousal regulation techniques, and they are all helpful for making sure that hockey players are in the best state of mind to play.

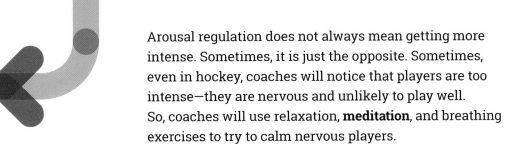

ALL IN THE MIND

Sidney Crosby: The Art of Trickery

As a **rookie** in the 2005–2006 season, Sidney Crosby of the Pittsburgh Penguins was weak at face-offs. He set about trying to improve his record of winning face-offs, and by 2010, he had made much progress.

No longer a rookie, in a game in December 2016, he faced the Phoenix Coyotes' Lauri Korpikoski. Korpikoski replaced Vernon Fiddler for the face-off after Fiddler was pulled from the face-off for slashing at Crosby's hands. Crosby knew that Korpikoski, having been pulled into the face-off at the last minute, would be distracted. Crosby expected him to bear down in his focus on winning the face-off. Crosby was right—Korpikoski bore down, and in doing so gave away his planned strategy to move the puck back toward his goaltender. Crosby read the situation and Korpikoski's intention. He won the face-off by adjusting his strategy.

CHAPTER 4

OFFENSIVE Strategies

Like every team sport, hockey is a game of strategy. On the ice, it may look like a lot of speed and sometimes a lot of fighting, but really, there is strategy behind much of what you see.

FAKING

Faking is a strategy used in many sports. Soccer players fake when attempting to dribble the ball around an opponent, or they may fake before passing. Basketball players fake as they move the ball down the court, or they may fake a shot just before passing the ball to another player to take a shot. Quarterbacks in football may fake a pass to a wide receiver and, instead, hand the ball off to a running back.

When two players face off, they may try to fake each other out on the ice.

This hockey player looks poised to pass the puck—but is she?

In hockey, fakes often occur when an offensive player is trying to move the puck past the defense. A player may drop a shoulder to indicate movement in one direction, then skate around the defensive player in the other direction. Or, the player may fake a pass to another player, but then, the moment the defensive player puts themselves in position to stop the pass, skate around the defensive player and continue down the ice. In either case, fakes in hockey work best if the player with the puck performs the fake outside of the reach of the defender's stick.

CREATING AN ATTACK TRIANGLE

Another offensive tactic is the attack triangle, which is where the offensive player passes the puck through the defensive player's legs. The offensive player pulls the puck wide to one side of the defender, so that the defender will lunge toward it—in doing so, the defender naturally spreads his legs apart a little to gain stability. That creates a "triangle" through which the offensive player can then pass the puck. The offensive player then skates around the defensive player and picks up the puck on the defender's other side. This all takes place in a split second, but it can be a very effective offensive strategy.

When heading toward the goal, an offensive player may pass the puck through a defender's legs and pick it up on the other side—moving ever closer to a shot at the goal.

PASSING OFF THE BOARDS

Somewhat similar to an attack triangle, passing off the boards allows an offensive player to pass the puck to himself. In an attack triangle play, the offensive player passes the puck through a defender's legs and picks it up on the other side. When passing off the boards, an offensive player facing a defender near the edges of the ice, can chip the puck off the boards, causing it to bounce back onto the ice *behind* the defensive player. The offensive player can tap the puck to chip it off the boards and skate around the defensive player, picking up the puck on his other side. It is a simple, but effective technique.

USING THE CROSS AND DROP

Another useful offensive strategy is the cross and drop. The player with the puck skates in front of another offensive player and "drops" the puck for the second player to pick up. The second player grabs the puck and moves forward quickly. Meanwhile, the defender tries to adjust their defense, since they have to switch rapidly from defending against one player to defending against the player who picked up the dropped puck.

USING DEFLECTION TO SCORE

Hockey offensive strategy is all about scoring. The offensive team's goal is to move the puck across the ice and score in the defending team's goal. This sounds easy because there are only five players defending at any given time—and sometimes, there are fewer than five, if one or more players is on a penalty. However, it is actually not easy, since the defending team will try to get the offensive players offside whenever possible. The offense has to be sure to watch the defense and predict when they are going to try to move into a position that puts the players offside.

When the puck in deflected, offensive players watch for opportunities to score.

Once the offense gets the puck down near the goal, they can try to shoot it. However, a good goalie will be able to stop most shots. So, one strategy the offense can use is to get a **deflection** for a goal. In this strategy, the team takes a shot at the goal, which the goalie deflects. When the puck comes back out of the goal, another offensive player then tries to shoot it into the goal before the goalie has a chance to react.

CHECKING: BRAIN OR BRAWN?

MIND VS. MUSCLE

Checking is probably the most common defensive strategy in hockey. Checking is making contact with another player's body or stick to try and gain control of the puck. There are different types of check, and they all try to disrupt the player who has the puck, so that the player performing the check can get control of the puck.

On the surface, checking looks like a brawn move. A player is slamming into another player to try to throw them off balance. In reality, though, there is strategy behind it. Even if the player checking another player does not end up gaining control of the puck, they have slowed down the player with the puck. In that way, it is a good defense strategy, even if control of the puck does not end up changing.

As brutal as it may look, checking is actually a strategic move in many cases.

The goalie often spends the entire game in the goal, but this is not always the case.

PULLING THE GOALIE

The goaltender is a team's number-one defender, so it may seem strange that the goalie can become a team's attack weapon! If the game is nearing the end, the team that is behind may decide to pull their goalie out of the goal and replace them with a forward. This gives the team an extra offensive player to try to score. It is a risky move, because it leaves the goal undefended, but it can pay off—to come back from behind, they need all the chances to score they can get.

CHAPTER 5

DEFENSIVE STRATEGIES

Offense is the name of the game in hockey, since scoring is how a team wins the game. However, defense is equally important, because no matter how good a team is, if the opposing team can score, it is not likely to win.

USING THE OFFSIDE RULE

Every player on the hockey team is responsible for defense. The goalie is the last line of defense. If the offense gets past every player and takes a shot at the goal, it is up to the goalie to stop it.

Since the goalie is the last in the line of defense, it is a better strategy never to let the puck and the offense get to the goalie. If there is any way for the rest of the team to keep the offense from getting a shot at the goal, they will. One way players do so is by making the offside rule work for them whenever possible.

If an offensive player crosses the blue line before the puck does, they are offside.

The defensive team will sometimes try to lure the offense into an offside position to force a face-off.

An offensive player is offside if they enter the attacking zone before the puck does. In other words, a player from the offensive team cannot skate into the attacking zone and simply wait there for someone to pass the puck to them, so they can take a shot at the goal. The puck has to enter the attacking zone first.

If an offside call happens, the puck is placed at the closest neutral face-off place to where the offside infraction happened. One player from each team then faces off to try to gain control of the puck.

If an offensive team is closing in on the goal, the defensive team may try to force an offside call by deliberately putting one (or more) of the offensive players into an offside position. That way, the defense has a chance at getting control of the puck back if they win the face-off. Even if they do not, the puck is back in neutral territory, which is probably farther from the goal than it was.

CREATING A NEUTRAL ZONE TRAP

When a team is stronger on defense than offense, it may decide to try creating a neutral zone trap. This is where the defense of a team creates a block, so that the offense of the opposing team cannot make it out of the neutral zone and into the attacking zone. Generally, the defensive team will put four players in the neutral zone and one into the other team's attacking zone. That one player in the attacking zone will force the other team's offense toward the sides of the ice by cutting off passing zones to other players. The other four players will continue to guard the other players, making sure they never get out of the neutral zone.

Teams with strong defense may make use of the neutral zone and not allow offensive players into the attacking zone.

ALL IN THE MIND

Kirk McLean: Confidence in the Goal

Being a goaltender is incredibly stressful. The pressure to stop the puck from sailing into the net is tremendous. However, former goaltender, Kirk McLean, was always calm under pressure. In a game in 1994 for the Vancouver Canucks, he stopped an incredible 52 goals!

Coach Mike Keenan of the New York Rangers was quick to point out the strength of McLean's confidence when the Rangers were set to face Vancouver in their next game. Confidence brings more confidence, Keenan said, and Kirk McLean's confidence was strong after that career-making game.

Keenan told the Rangers that their best strategy against McLean, the confident goalie, was to try to distract him. Distraction could equal goals scored, and then McLean's confidence would crumble. It worked: The Rangers ended up winning the game 3 to 1.

COMBINING DEFENSE STRATEGIES

In many sports, man-to-man defense is popular. In this defense, each defensive player guards one player on the opposing team. Another defensive strategy commonly used in many sports is zone defense, where each defensive player guards a particular zone on the field or the court.

Teams have to work together to come up with a strong defensive strategy.

However, hockey moves too fast for either of these types of defense to be extremely effective. Man-to-man defense, in particular, is difficult to accomplish well in hockey. So, some teams have begun to use a combination of the two defensive strategies. Two or three players will be assigned players on the opposing team for man-to-man defense, and the remaining players on the team will cover zone defense. It can be a slightly chaotic method of covering defense, but in a fast-moving game like hockey, it works fairly well.

USING THE ICING RULE

Another defensive strategy hockey teams use is the rule of icing. Icing is when a player shoots the puck across the center red line and the opposing team's goal line, with no players touching the puck as it crosses those two lines. In other words, the player shoots the puck more than halfway down the rink, past the other team's goal line.

Often, players keep the puck close to them, but sometimes they will shoot it across the rink, and icing may occur.

Body contact is not only allowed in hockey, it is the norm. Players expect a rough, fast-paced game every time they enter the rink.

This strategy is legal if the puck makes it into the goal—in that case, the offensive team scores a goal. It is not legal if the puck simply sails down the ice and past the goal line, but not into the goal. Legal or not, though, icing is a way to waste time and tire out the other team. If the defense of one team keeps sending the puck to the other end of the rink, the offensive team then has to skate after it and return. It takes time, and it is tiring.

If the defense is short a player (because they are on a penalty, which is very common in hockey), then icing is legal. In that case, it is not only a time-waster, but it is also a legal one.

If a team chooses to ice the puck even when it is not legal, the referee will call a face-off in the defensive zone of the team that iced the puck. As long as the team is pretty confident its player will win the face-off, then it is a worthwhile strategy to use.

CHAPTER 6

GAME-DAY

Ready!

All the practice, **drills**, and hard work are in preparation for the big game. When that day comes, players must be ready both physically and mentally, as each player's skill and focus will be tested. There are a number of strategies players can use to prepare themselves mentally to perform their best.

REGULATING AROUSAL

Hockey is an intense game, and players need to have a certain level of intensity to keep up on the ice. However, too much intensity can cause a player to be distracted and not play well. So, sports psychologists can help hockey players learn arousal regulation techniques that can get them to the right level of intensity for the big game.

Meditation can help hockey players regulate their arousal, so that they do not become too intense on the ice.

Arousal regulation techniques differ from player to player. Some players may get themselves pumped up by listening to upbeat music or by watching recordings of past games where they played at their peak. Others may find that using affirmations gets them ready for a game.

If a player is feeling too intense and needs to relax, they might try listening to some calming music. Some may practice meditation, which can help them relax. Deep breathing is another useful technique for calming the body.

TALKING IT UP

Affirmations are a common tool that psychologists use in many areas. In sports psychology, affirmations usually involve a player repeating positive statements to themselves. For example, a goalie might repeat daily, "I am the best player in the league at blocking goals. I stop more goals than any other player on the ice."

This may be a little overstatement, but the point is, that if a player repeats an affirmation enough, they will begin to believe it. That then brings confidence. As New York Rangers coach Mike Keenan rightfully pointed out, confidence brings more confidence. And more confidence brings better play. So, even if an affirmation might be a little on the boastful side, the important thing is that it brings confidence to the player.

Smart hockey players will set manageable goals for themselves.

SETTING GOALS

Sports psychologists also encourage players to set short, achievable goals. Bigger, long-term goals are useful, too. Thinking, "Someday, I want to be known as a better player than Wayne Gretzky," is not harmful in any way. However, that is a very big goal that is difficult to reach. So, sports psychologists recommend that players also make smaller goals that they can work toward.

Perhaps a player will set a goal of scoring one more goal in each game they play: If the player scored one goal in the previous game, their goal will be to score two goals in the next game, then three goals, and so on. These types of goal are much more easily reached, and when they are reached, they bring confidence to the player. And confidence brings about better overall play.

MIND vs. MUSCLE

WOMEN IN HOCKEY

It wasn't until 1998 that the Winter Olympics held its first women's ice hockey tournament. Even today, hockey is a very male-dominated sport. But women now compete in the game at all levels, from youth leagues all the way to the professional level. In the United States, the National Women's Hockey League (NWHL) began its first season in 2015. Today, women's hockey leagues are still growing and becoming more and more popular.

Some coaches find their motivational strategies are different depending on whether they are coaching male or female athletes. Both male and female players tend to react best when there is respect between the coaches and the players. Good communication is also a key to success. Olympian Karen Thatcher says women often want to know why a coach is asking something, and they tend to respond better when they feel as if the coach respects them both on the ice and off the ice.

Thatcher also says that when coaching female hockey players, embarrassment is never a smart technique. Some coaches use this as a strategy to motivate a player to do better, but Thatcher says it can cause more harm than good with female players. A better strategy, Thatcher says, is explaining to players what they did poorly and giving examples for how they can improve next time they are on the ice.

Coaches recognize the value of using the right techniques to motivate individual players.

Players who visualize winning or performing well often find that they perform better during a game.

VISUALIZING THE OUTCOME

Visualization is a very commonly used technique in sports psychology. Players are encouraged to visualize the outcomes they want to happen. For example, an offensive player might visualize shooting the puck into the goal. A goalie might visualize stopping every puck that comes flying across the ice or through the air into the goal. The goalie might visualize performing pad stops and catching the puck using his catch glove.

Seeing is believing, and when a player visualizes a certain outcome, they will eventually start to believe it on some level. Their body will "remember" performing the shot or save and will naturally try to do it again. It is also a confidence-building technique. Players "see" themselves playing well through visualizations, and it builds their confidence and improves their play.

A GAME OF WITS

Hockey is known as a game of physical contact and brawn, but it is also a game of skill and strategy. As the puck and the players move quickly on the ice, the players are constantly looking over the situation and planning their next move. Are they going to check the player who has the puck? Ice the puck? Set up to shoot at the goal? Try to put the offense on offside? It all depends who has the puck and where the game is going.

The best hockey players take this all in and make quick decisions based on what they see on the ice. They will also use sports psychology techniques to make sure they are playing at the top of their game. They will be sure that their mind and their body are ready to play at peak performance.

Coaches use sports psychology techniques to make sure the players on their team are playing at their very best. For a team to be on top, all players need to be playing at their peak. Coaches know that, and they will use both physical practice and mental strategy to coax the best performance out of their team.

A team is as good as its players—together, a confident and focused team can win the game.

GLOSSARY

arousal regulation managing a person's level of intensity, which can range from most relaxed (sleeping) to most excited, through the use of different exercises and techniques

athleticism strength, fitness, and agility in an athlete

carotid artery a main artery that carries blood to the head and neck

composite made up of different parts or elements

deflection causing something to reverse direction

drills practice exercises that are repeated over and over

face-off when two players on opposing teams stand at a spot on the ice and a puck is dropped between them; whoever gets it first gains control of the puck for their team

garters bands worn around the legs to hold up socks

goal setting setting small, manageable goals to achieve an overall greater goal

hash marks a series of parallel marks

icing shooting the puck from one end of the ice rink to another without letting the puck enter the goal

intensity strong feeling or emotion

internalize to make an attitude or behavior part of one's own nature

jugular vein a major vein in the neck

logo an identifying symbol

meditation a relaxation technique in which one reflects carefully on thoughts

offside moving into the attacking zone on a hockey rink before the puck does

radius a straight line running from the center of a circle to the circumference

rookie a beginner player who does not have a lot of experience

self-talk words or phrases a person says to themselves to be more effective in reaching a goal

solar plexus the area that includes a complex system of nerves on the front of the body just below the ribs, at the pit of the stomach

subculture a culture or group within a larger culture or group

triceps the large muscle at the back of the upper arm

visualization forming a mental image of an action or object

FOR MORE INFORMATION

BOOKS

Biskup, Agnieszka. *Hockey: How It Works*. Mankato, MN: Capstone Press, 2010.

Frederick, Shane. *The Best of Everything Hockey Book*. Mankato, MN: Capstone Press, 2011.

Herman, Gail. *Who Is Wayne Gretzky?* New York, NY: Grosset & Dunlap, 2015.

Nagelhout, Ryan. *The Science of Hockey*. New York, NY: PowerKids Press, 2016.

WEBSITES

Find out about health, sports, and fitness at:
www.brainpop.com/health/sportsandfitness

For more information about hockey, check out:
www.ducksters.com/sports/hockey.php

Test your knowledge of hockey and math on this NHL page:
www.futuregoals.nhl.com/future-goals-stem-module

Sports Illustrated Kids has all the latest news at:
www.sikids.com

INDEX